from a C̶̶̶̶̶ ̶̶̶̶ ̶̶̶̶ Perspective

by
Roy Schoeman

*All booklets are published thanks to the
generous support of the members of the
Catholic Truth Society*

CATHOLIC TRUTH SOCIETY
PUBLISHERS TO THE HOLY SEE

Contents

Why Judaism?

There are many reasons why a Catholic might want to learn about any of the other world religions. In addition to all of these, there is a very special reason for a Catholic to learn about Judaism. For the relationship between Judaism and the Catholic Church is absolutely unique. As Pope John Paul II put it:

> "The Jewish religion is not 'extrinsic' to us, but in a certain way is 'intrinsic' to our own religion. With Judaism, therefore, we have a relationship which we do not have with any other religion. You [i.e. the Jews] are our dearly beloved brothers and, in a certain way, it could be said that you are our elder brothers."[1] "Jesus belongs to the Jewish people, and he inaugurated his church within the Jewish nation.[2] ...Whoever meets Jesus Christ, meets Judaism".[3]

From a Christian perspective, Judaism and Christianity are actually one and the same religion, divided into two phases, one designed for the period leading up to the Incarnation of Christ, the other for the period following. Thus Judaism is "pre-Messianic

Christianity", and the Church "post-Messianic Judaism".
In the words of Vatican II:

> In carefully planning and preparing the salvation of
> the whole human race the God of infinite love, by a
> special dispensation, chose for Himself a people to
> whom He would entrust His promises. First He
> entered into a covenant with Abraham and, through
> Moses, with the people of Israel...The plan of
> salvation foretold by the sacred authors, recounted
> and explained by them, is found as the true word of
> God in the books of the Old Testament...The
> principal purpose to which the plan of the old
> covenant was directed was to prepare for the
> coming of Christ, the redeemer of all and of the
> messianic kingdom, to announce this coming by
> prophecy, and to indicate its meaning through
> various types.[4] [T]he books of the Old Testament
> with all their parts...acquire and show forth their full
> meaning in the New Testament and in turn shed
> light on it and explain it.[5]

Given this link, the Council Fathers expressed the
Church's special debt to the Jewish people:

> [T]his sacred council remembers the spiritual ties
> which link the people of the new covenant to the
> stock of Abraham. The church of Christ

acknowledges that in God's plan of salvation the beginnings of its faith and election are to be found in the patriarchs, Moses and the prophets...and that the salvation of the church is mystically prefigured in the exodus of God's chosen people from the land of bondage. On this account the church cannot forget that it received the revelation of the Old Testament by way of that people with whom God in his inexpressible mercy established the ancient covenant. Nor can it forget that it draws nourishment from that good olive tree onto which the wild olive branches of the Gentiles have been grafted (*Rm* 11:17-24). The church... is mindful, moreover, that the apostles, the pillars on which the church stands, are of Jewish descent, as are many of those early disciples who proclaimed the Gospel of Christ to the world...[6]

In many ways, the Church's history, theology, and even liturgy flows from its pre-Messianic, that is its Jewish, roots. Therefore for a Catholic, Judaism comes alive when seen through the eyes of the Catholic faith, and Catholic faith and practice takes on even more depth, meaning, and beauty when seen in its relationship to Judaism.

The Jewish Religion

To understand Judaism, it is helpful to consider it as a people, a faith, and a covenant.

A People

Judaism represents a single people, or tribe - the descendents of Abraham, the father of the Jews, through his son Isaac. Of course, over the 4000 years since Abraham there has been conversion into, as well as, out of Judaism, and extensive intermarriage and intermingling of people, but Jewish people's identity as the "seed of Abraham" remains as a central theological principle of Judaism.

As a result, Judaism has never considered itself as appropriate for all peoples, and the evangelization of non-Jews has never been a priority. Rather, it represents a covenant made by God to a single people, for the special role that that people were to play among all the nations of the earth. Judaism sees the Jews as having been specially chosen by God to live in a uniquely close relationship with Him, not just for their own sakes, but to intercede for the rest of humanity as a "priestly people"("You shall be to me a kingdom of priests and a holy nation" - Exodus 19:4), bringing the knowledge of God, and His blessings, to the whole world ("I have given you as a covenant to the people, a light to the nations" - Isaiah 42:6). As a leading rabbi recently wrote:

> "The Jew is a creature of heaven and of earth, of a heavenly Divine soul which is truly a part of Godliness clothed in an earthly vessel...whose purpose is to realize the transcendence and unity of his nature and of the world in which he lives within the absolute unity of God. The realization of this purpose entails a two-way correlation: one in the direction from above downward to earth; the other, from the earth upward. In fulfillment of the first, man draws holiness from the Divinely given Torah and commandments, to permeate therewith every phase of his daily life and environment; in fulfillment of the second, man draws upon all the resources at this disposal as vehicles for his personal ascendancy and, with him, that of the surrounding world."[7]

This self-understanding as a special people chosen for a special vocation often leads Jews to place a primary emphasis on maintaining their separate identity.

A Covenant

Judaism is based on the special covenant that God made with Abraham and his descendants through the generations. The story is told in Genesis 12-22, contained in both the Christian and the Jewish Bible. About 2000 years before Christ, when all the peoples of the earth were pagans, worshiping a host of false gods and idols (which were in fact fallen spirits, or demons - "the gods of the pagans are demons", *Ps* 96:5), the one true God revealed Himself to one of the pagans, Abram (later renamed Abraham) and asked him to travel to a distant land, where God would make him the father of a great people. After Abraham demonstrated his fidelity through a series of tests, culminating in his willingness to sacrifice his only legitimate son to God, God rewarded Abraham with the promise of a special blessing on his seed, and that through them all the peoples of the earth would be blessed:

> "I have sworn, says the LORD, because you have done this, and have not withheld your son, your only son, I will indeed bless you, and I will multiply your descendants as the stars of heaven and as the sand which is on the seashore. And your descendants shall possess the gate of their enemies, and by your descendants shall all the nations of the earth be blessed, because you have obeyed my voice." (*Gn* 22:16-18).

This was the origin of the Jewish people, of the special covenant God made with them, and of God's promise to one day send, through them, the Messiah, to establish God's reign on earth.

A Faith

The Jewish Scriptures

God continued His special relationship with Abraham's son, Isaac, Isaac's son Jacob (later renamed Israel, hence the use of "Israel" to refer to the Jewish people), and Jacob's sons, who became the patriarchs of the twelve tribes of Israel. During a time of famine, Jacob and his sons moved to Egypt, where they were later made slaves. One of them, Moses, was appointed by God to be their liberator. Moses led the Jews out of their captivity in Egypt and through the desert to the "promised land", then called Canaan, later called Israel. During the journey through the Sinai God appeared to Moses on Mount Sinai and gave him the first five books of the Bible, that Judaism calls the "Torah", or "Law." The Torah became the cornerstone of the Jewish faith. Over the succeeding centuries, revelations made to other Jewish prophets were accepted as of Divine Origin and added to the original Torah to make up the Old Testament, which Jews call the "Tanakh". Tanakh is a Hebrew word made up of the initial consonants of the three words "Torah", or "law", the five books revealed to Moses on Mt. Sinai; "Nevi'im", or "prophets", referring to the revelations given to the prophets; and "K'tuvim", or "writings", which refers to the wisdom literature such as the books of Psalms, Proverbs, etc. The Jewish Old Testament in its entirety is accepted as Divine Revelation by the Catholic Church.

The Jewish canon of scripture - that is, the exact collection of books to be considered Sacred Scripture and included in the Tanakh - has varied from century to century and place to place. A few hundred years before Christ, a compilation of such writings were collected and translated into Greek for use by the Jews, many of whom no longer understood Hebrew. This Greek language version of the Jewish Old Testament is known as the Septuagint.

Later, however, a number of books contained in the Septuagint were eliminated from the Jewish canon. When the Temple in Jerusalem was destroyed in 70 AD and the Jews expelled from that city, the leading rabbis regrouped in the town of Jamnia, which became the center of Jewish learning. There, in the beginning of the second century AD, it was decided that the more recently written books of the Septuagint should be excluded from the canon. The reason for this is unclear, but since it was done by the same rabbis who condemned the New Testament and Jewish followers of Jesus, some think it was done to purify Judaism from the taint of Christianity.

The Catholic canon of the Old Testament includes those books dropped from the Jewish canon at Jamnia, while the Protestant canon of the Old Testament rejects them. It is hard to see why a decision made by Jewish authorities decades after the Church was formed should be considered relevant for the Church, especially when made by the same authorities who anathematized Christians and condemned the writings of the New Testament.

The final stage in the development of the Jewish scriptures took place between the third and the sixth century after Christ, when Jewish authorities wrote down the oral tradition that had developed within Judaism. This became known as the Talmud, or "teaching". It is the record of discussions and exegesis by leading rabbis over the generations, and is granted an authority within Judaism comparable to that of the Old Testament.

A Jewish Creed

The closest that Judaism comes to an official creed is the "Thirteen Principles of Faith" of Moses Maimonides (1135-1204), the primary Jewish sage of the middle ages. They serve as a good introduction to the central tenets of the Jewish faith.

The first five of the principles revolve around the heart of the Jewish faith - the belief in, and fidelity to, the one true, uncreated, creator God (in particular contrast to the polytheistic pagan idol worship of those around them in the times of the Old Testament). They are:

1. God is the Creator and Ruler of all things. He alone has made, does make, and will make all things.
2. God is One. There is no unity that is in any way like His. He alone is our God. He was, He is, and He will be.
3. God does not have a body. Physical concepts do not apply to Him. There is nothing whatsoever that resembles Him at all.
4. God is first and last.
5. One may only pray to God. One may not pray to anyone or anything else.

The next four of the principles assert the truth, divine origin, and immutability of the Jewish Scriptures:

6. All the words of the prophets are true.
7. The prophecy of Moses is absolutely true. He was the chief of all prophets, both before and after Him.
8. The entire Torah that we now have is that which was given to Moses.
9. This Torah will not be changed, and there will never be another given by God.

The next two are:

10. God knows all of man's deeds and thoughts. It is thus written (*Ps* 33:15), "He has molded every heart together, He understands what each one does."
11. God rewards those who keep His commandments, and punishes those who transgress Him.

These reflect the belief in God's absolute sovereignty, omniscience, and omnipotence, which is central to Judaism. He knows and sees all things ("You know my resting and my rising, you discern my purpose from afar." *Ps* 139:2). He has given the Jewish people, as his special priestly people, an extensive body of law, much of which applies only to them, that will be a source of peace, happiness, and blessing to them if they obey it. If they fail to, they will be punished.

Judaism expects, in general, that the reward or punishment for good or bad behavior will occur in this life, as well as in the next. The central prayer of Judaism, recited three times a day, is the "Shema", drawn from Deuteronomy 11, which promises temporal good fortune as a reward for obedience to God:

> If you obey My commandments that I command you...then will I send the rain for your land in its season... And I will provide grass in your field for your cattle, and you shall eat and be sated. Be careful that your heart be not tempted and you turn away to serve other gods and bow to them. For then God will be furious with you and will block the heavens and there will be no rain and the land will not yield its produce, and you will perish quickly from the good land that God gives you. (*Dt* 11:13-17)

Of course, Judaism also recognizes a mystery behind suffering, and that at times the good suffer too (e.g. the story of Job). But there is no well-developed theology of the redemptive value of suffering in Judaism, or in the Old Testament, comparable to what is found in Christianity. This is only logical, from a Christian viewpoint, since it was only with the coming of Christ that suffering took on its ultimate redemptive value, through one's uniting it with the suffering of Christ.

The next of Maimonides' principles reflects the Jewish faith in the coming of the promised Messiah, who will establish God's reign on earth:

12. The Messiah will come. However long it takes, I will await His coming every day.

The belief in the coming of the Messiah is absolutely central to traditional Judaism (although in recent times the more modern forms of Judaism have moved away from this belief). The Old Testament contains hundreds of prophecies relating to the Messiah that detail who he will be, of what lineage, where and when he will be born, what he will do, how he will transform the world, and so forth.[8] Many of them are, however, somewhat mysterious or veiled in nature.

There is also some apparent contradiction between them - in particular, some seem to predict a Messiah who will come to suffer and die in atonement for the sins of the people (e.g. the Suffering Servant passage in Isaiah 53), while others portray a Messiah who will come in victory to restore the glory of the Israel and establish a kingdom of peace and prosperity on earth (*Is* 11, 25).

This apparent contradiction is the topic of extensive discussion in the Talmud, which concludes that there will be, in fact, two Messiahs, one who will come to suffer and die (referred to in the Talmud as "Messiah son of Joseph"), and one who would come in victory ("Messiah son of David"). This view mirrors quite closely the Christian resolution of the same apparent contradiction, which recognizes some of the Messianic prophecies as referring to Christ's First Coming (to suffer and die), and others to his return in glory at the Second Coming.

The traditional Jewish liturgy contains prayers for the coming of the Messiah during daily morning, afternoon, and evening prayers.

The final principle of faith is:

13. The dead will be brought back to life when God wills it to happen.

Judaism has a much less well developed theology of the afterlife than does Christianity, as this principle reflects. The general sense in the Old Testament (typified in the Book of Job) is that there is an eternal life which entails reward and punishment, but the details are best left in the hands of God. (This uncertainty in Judaism about the afterlife is reflected in the New Testament in the disputes between the Pharisees and the Sadducees on just this issue - *Mt* 22, *Mk* 12, *Lk* 20, *Ac* 23). Although there is discussion of both heaven and hell in the Talmud, it leaves room for a variety of opinions on heaven, hell, the resurrection, and even reincarnation.

From a Christian perspective it makes sense that the Jewish scriptures - revelations made to man before Christ - should be vague about the afterlife, since according to Christianity, before Christ descended to the dead after the crucifixion, there were no human souls in heaven. Rather, the souls of the just were consigned to a shadowy underworld, the "limbo of the fathers", awaiting His coming to open the gates of Heaven.

Jewish Laws

One distinguishing characteristic of Judaism is the emphasis on following a wide range of ritual laws. Traditional Judaism identifies 613 commandments in the Old Testament, which in aggregate dictate one's behavior in almost every aspect of life. Many of these laws require further elucidation and specification - for instance, what constitutes the sort of "work" that is prohibited on the Sabbath? This elucidation is provided, sometimes at great length, in the Talmud.

From a Jewish perspective, this ritual law is natural and intrinsic to the role of the Jews as a "priestly nation". It is natural that as such, every aspect of their lives is to be consecrated to God. A Catholic can see this as roughly analogous to the difference in the manner of life of an ordinary Christian, or one in religious life, i.e. a monk or nun. It is as though every Jew is called, in Jewish law, to follow the sort of strict regime of laws that characterize

Catholic religious life, especially as it was in past centuries, when almost every aspect of how a religious ate, dressed, behaved, spoke, slept, worked and prayed was dictated by a rule. The rule was a way for the religious to consecrate every aspect of his life to God. That is how Jewish ritual observance, which permeates every aspect of the religious Jew's life, is to be understood.

In the realm of eating, the laws define the foods one is, or is not, allowed to eat; how the animal must be slaughtered; what foods may not be eaten together; and how one is to purify himself prior to eating. They define how one is to dress, the wearing of special clothing with ritual significance (e.g. a head covering at all times, and the "tzitzit", or fringes, on the corners of the garment[9]), what fabrics can be worn and in what combination. They define various aspects of personal grooming - for instance, forbidding men from shaving or cutting the hair on their temples, hence the traditional beards and earlocks of strictly observant Jews.[10] They define whom one is or is not allowed to touch, how the Sabbath and festivals are to be observed, how and when one is to pray, and so forth.

Many of these laws may appear arbitrary, foolish, or rude to non-Jews. Yet most come directly from the Old Testament and so the Christian must recognize them as having been commanded of the Jews by God. It was only when Christ came that these laws were lifted from the Jews- they were never commanded of the Gentiles - as described in the New Testament (e.g. *Mt* 15, *Ac* 10, *Rm* 14). Of course, since Judaism rejects the authority of the New Testament, it considers the laws still binding.

Rabbinic and Temple Judaism

There are nonetheless great differences between today's Judaism and the Judaism that is presented in the Old Testament, especially around the role of animal sacrifice. These changes were necessitated by the destruction of the Temple in Jerusalem in 70 AD. The sacramental system prescribed for the Jews in the Old Testament required animal sacrifice that had to be performed in one place, the Temple in Jerusalem. Animals were to be sacrificed daily - for the remission of sins, for purification, for atonement, and as thanksgiving. When the Temple was destroyed and those sacrifices were no longer possible, the leading rabbis of the day gathered in Jamnia, which at the time served as the seat of Jewish learning (the Jews had been expelled from Jerusalem under pain of death by the Romans), and developed as an alternative the current system, known as "Rabbinic" Judaism (as opposed to the earlier form, "Temple" Judaism), in which prayers, almsgivings, and good deeds are substituted for the no longer possible animal sacrifice.

The Jewish Liturgical Year

Judaism strives to consecrate every aspect of the Jew's life to God - through obedience to the laws, through prayer, and through the observance of the Jewish liturgical year. Home observances, as opposed to sacraments that take place outside the home, are the heart and soul of Jewish religious life. These observances are driven by the regular cycles of the Jewish liturgical year.

The Weekly Sabbath

The basic rhythm of Jewish religious life is set by the weekly Sabbath. The Sabbath begins shortly before sundown on Friday, and ends with nightfall the next day. During that period, all "work" is forbidden, which for observant Jews includes riding in a car or other vehicle, buying or selling, lighting a fire, turning on electric lights or appliances (hence no television, radio, etc.), walking any significant distance, carrying anything, sports activities, writing, cooking, gardening, or doing any secular work.

Sabbath observance traditionally starts with the woman of the house lighting the Sabbath candles shortly before sundown on Friday, followed by an elaborate meal that is accompanied with special prayers and blessings. The following day is devoted to synagogue worship, religious study, and family activities. The religious and family orientation of the day is ensured by the Sabbath observance laws, which prohibit most of the activities which might tend to draw family members apart, or to inject a worldly element into the day. The Sabbath is so observed in fulfillment of the commandment found in Exodus 20:

> "Remember the Sabbath day, to keep it holy. Six days you shall labor, and do all your work; but the seventh day is a Sabbath to the LORD your God; in it you shall not do any work...for in six days the LORD made heaven and earth, the sea, and all that is in them, and rested the seventh day; therefore the LORD blessed the Sabbath day and made it holy."

Sabbath ends on Saturday evening with the Havdala ceremony which makes use of a special multi-wicked candle, a spice box, and wine, along with special prayers and blessings, to conclude the Sabbath.

The Festivals

Most of the Jewish festivals share the same restrictions on "work" as the Sabbath, and much of their celebration and observance takes place in the home, often accompanied with special foods, objects, or activities unique to the feast. A brief description of some of the major holidays follows:

Rosh Hashanah "New Year" & Yom Kippur "Day of Atonement"

These two holidays are separated by ten days, and usually fall in September or October. Rosh Hashanah is considered the anniversary of God's creation of the world, and it is the day that God looks at the deeds of each individual to determine their destiny for the coming year. This sobering prospect is reflected in a central prayer of Rosh Hashanah, the "U'Netaneh Tokef" ("How utterly holy this day is"):

> All will pass before You like members of the flock. Like a shepherd pasturing his flock, making sheep pass under his staff, so shall You cause to pass, count, calculate, and consider the soul of all the living; and You shall apportion the fixed needs of all Your creatures and inscribe their verdict.

> On Rosh Hashanah will be inscribed and on Yom Kippur will be sealed how many will pass from the earth and how many will be created; who will live and who will die; who will die at his predestined time and who before his time; who by water and who by fire, who by sword, who by beast, who by

famine, who by thirst, who by storm, who by plague, who by strangulation, and who by stoning. Who will rest and who will wander, who will live in harmony and who will be harried, who will enjoy tranquility and who will suffer, who will be impoverished and who will be enriched, who will be degraded and who will be exalted.

Since the verdict will be inscribed on Rosh Hashanah and sealed on Yom Kippur, the ten days between the two holidays are an intense time of prayer, almsgiving, and reconciliation aimed at averting the "severe decree" before it is too late. They are known as the "ten days of Repentance".

Yom Kippur serves as the climax of this period of repentance. It is observed as a strict fast day, with no food or water being taken from sundown to sundown (in addition to fasting, also prohibited are wearing leather shoes, bathing or washing, anointing oneself with oil, and marital relations). Most of the day is spent in the synagogue praying the most solemn liturgy of the year. When the Temple still stood in Jerusalem (it was destroyed for the final time in 70 AD), Yom Kippur was the one and only day of the year that the High Priest entered the Holy of Holies, making atonement for the sins of the Jewish nation as well as his own. Today's Yom Kippur liturgy still reflects that unique solemnity.

Sukkot

Sukkot (or "booths"), falls four days after Yom Kippur and lasts one week. It is one of the most joyful holidays of the year. It celebrates the harvest, and also commemorates the forty-year period during which the Jews wandered in the desert following the Exodus from Egypt, living in temporary shelters. In observance of this, during Sukkot observant Jews live in temporary shelters ("Sukkot", or "booths") outside the home, and work is prohibited on the first and second days. The observance of the holiday was directly commanded by God in the Old Testament (*Lv* 23).

Hanukkah

The eight-day festival of Hanukkah begins on the 25th of the month of Kislev on the Jewish calendar, which usually falls around Christmas. Originally a relatively minor holiday, it has assumed a much greater weight because of its proximity to Christmas, and the alternative it provides. The holiday is mentioned in 1st and 2nd Maccabees. It celebrates the victory of the Maccabees against the Emperor Antiochus who, after coming to power over the Jews, forced them to follow pagan practices, and desecrated the Temple. When the Maccabees defeated Antiochus they recaptured and rededicated the Temple, enabling the resumption of the sacrifices so central to the Jewish sacramental system.

As soon as they reconsecrated the Temple, the Maccabees relit the multi-branched lamp (Menorah) which was to burn uninterruptedly in the Temple. However, due to the just-ended war, only enough oil for a single day could be found. Miraculously, the oil lasted for eight days, until a new supply could be found. In commemoration, Hanukkah lasts for eight days, and a Menorah with eight branches is lit each evening - one candle the first night, two the second, and so forth, until on the last night all eight are lit. There are special prayers and songs for the lighting of the Menorah, and it is customary for children to receive gifts each night. There are also traditional foods and children's games associated with the holiday.

Passover

The Jews' "Exodus", their being freed from slavery to the Pharaoh in Egypt, is commemorated by an eight-day feast called "Passover". Passover is inaugurated by the Passover Seder, a festive meal in the home replete with special ritual foods, extensive prayers, and narrative thanking God for freeing the Jewish people from slavery in Egypt. Before the destruction of the Temple, the Passover meal included a lamb sacrificed in the Temple in commemoration of the lambs killed by the Jews just before their flight from Egypt, the blood of which was daubed on the doorposts of their houses to tell the angel of death to "pass over" the house[12] - hence "Passover". On the first and last day of the feast no work is to be done; during the entire 8-day period no leavened bread, or any forms of leavening, are to be eaten.

Shavuot (Pentecost)

Shavout falls on the fiftieth day after Passover. The name "Shavuot" literally means "sevens", for it falls seven weeks after Passover. It commemorates the giving of the Law to Moses on Mount Sinai; therefore many religious Jews observe the holiday by spending the entire night in Torah study, either at home or in synagogue.

Judaism Today

There are currently about 14 million Jews in the world today, or about two-tenths of one percent of the world population. Of these, about 6 million live in North America, 5 million in Israel, and 1 1/2 million in Europe. Their prominence is far disproportionate to their numbers. For instance, since the Nobel Prize was founded in 1901, over 20% of its winners (between 158 and 173, depending on the definition of being Jewish, out of 758) have been Jewish - in the sciences, almost 30%. Of course, within the Jewish community can be found a wide range of beliefs and practices.

"Orthodox" Judaism

Only a minority of Jews today attempt to follow the full range of Jewish law and observance, adhering to a strict interpretation of Jewish law and practices as they appear in the Old Testament and the Talmud. These are generally referred to as "orthodox Jews", and account for 10% of the Jews in the U.S., 17% of those in Israel.[13] In practice, Orthodox Jews, with the exception of the "ultra-Orthodox", described below, often live and work among non-Jews, but distinguish themselves by an observance of Jewish laws which set them apart. These laws include:

- a strict prohibition against working - which is defined as including driving, turning on an electric device, lighting a stove, etc. - on the Jewish Sabbath, which begins Friday at sunset and ends at sunset on Saturday.
- the requirement for men to keep their heads covered (hence the wearing of skullcaps)
- a prohibition against men shaving (although some interpret the law to allow electric shavers)
- strict dietary laws, such as the prohibition against eating any milk products and any meat products at the same meal, eating any unclean animal (defined in Leviticus 11 as including shellfish, pork, etc.), or any animal not properly slaughtered according to Jewish law (detailed in Leviticus 17).

The orthodox subscribe to the Jewish faith as described in the "13 Principles", including the belief in the coming of a Messiah, the rebuilding of the Temple in Jerusalem, and the resurrection of the dead. Their liturgy and religious study is conducted almost exclusively in Hebrew.

Within the orthodox is found smaller, even more observant, subgroup, known as Hasidim (3% of U.S. Jews, 5% of Jews living in Israel). They were founded in

Poland in the mid-18th century by Rabbi Israel ben Eliezer, known as the Baal Shem Tov ("Master of the Good Name"), who wished to put love of God at the center of Judaism, rather than the dry legalism that he saw around him. As he said, "I have come into this world to teach how to live by three precepts: love of God, love of Israel, and love of the Torah." Hasidic Judaism is characterized by a charismatic element. Their worship often involves joyful chanting, or even dancing, and some of their rabbis are famous for such charismatic gifts as the reading of souls, foreknowledge of events, and miracle working. Hasidic Jews follow a strict interpretation of traditional Jewish law, often living apart in separate communities under the authority of a rabbi. The strictness of their religious observance can limit their interaction with the outside world. Nonetheless, their numbers have doubled in the last twenty years, as a result both of their high birthrate and successful evangelization of non-Hasidic Jews, making them one of the fastest growing groups within Judaism.

"Reform" Judaism

Following the emancipation of the Jews in Germany in the 19th century, when Jews were for the first time accorded full civil rights, including the right to live and operate freely in the non-Jewish community, a liberalizing trend that came to be known as "Reform"

Judaism emerged, and soon spread throughout Western Europe and America. Its aim was to modernize Judaism by replacing the traditional Hebrew liturgy with one in the vernacular and make it more closely resemble Protestant services; allowing the individual to decide for himself what laws to follow; applying modern "higher criticism" to the understanding of scripture; replacing the tradition Jewish emphasis on ritual observance and worship with a concern for social justice: and embracing the customs, mores, and dress of modern culture. They account for 35% of U.S. Jews.

"Conservative" Judaism

In the late 19th century in Germany a countervailing movement emerged among Jews who wanted to participate fully in the modern world, and rejected the literal interpretation of Jewish scriptures and law, yet still wanted to conserve more of the Jewish tradition than the "Reform" movement did. Hence it came to be known as the "Conservative" movement. It falls in a middle ground between orthodox and Reform Judaism, mixing both Hebrew and the vernacular in the liturgy; adopting a historical-critical method in the interpretation of Jewish scripture and law; and adopting a positive attitude towards modern society. It accounts for 26% of U.S. Jews.

"Messianic" Jews/Jewish Converts[14]

Another, somewhat controversial, group to consider is Jews who recognize Jesus as the Jewish Messiah. Although most of them still consider themselves Jewish, usually the rest of the Jewish community does not. Some enter the Catholic Church or one of the conventional Protestant denominations, others remain separate in distinct "Messianic Jewish" congregations which maintain some of the traditional Jewish liturgical practices.

This group is growing - there may be more Jewish conversion to Christianity underway today than at any time since the early days of the Church. The statistics which exist are for Messianic Jews; their numbers may serve as a proxy for overall Jewish conversion. Before 1967, there were only a few thousand Messianic Jews in the U.S., and at most four or five Messianic Jewish synagogues[15] - today there are over 150. By the mid 1970's, Time magazine placed the number of Messianic Jews in the U.S. at over 50,000; by 1993 this number had grown to 160,000 in the U.S.[16] and over 350,000 worldwide. There are currently over 400 Messianic synagogues worldwide, including at least 150 in the U.S.

Of particular interest is the spread of Messianic Judaism in Israel itself. Despite opposition by the Israel government, there is now practically no town or city in

Israel without a "Messianic Jewish" congregation, and over 5000 Jewish converts to Christianity in Israel.[17] This cannot help but call to mind the prophecy that Jesus made when he sent his apostles out on their mission to evangelize (*Mt* 10:6-7, 23):

> [Go] to the lost sheep of the house of Israel. And preach as you go, saying, 'The kingdom of heaven is at hand.'... When they persecute you in one town, flee to the next; for truly, I say to you, you will not have gone through all the towns of Israel, before the Son of man comes.

Unaffiliated Jews

The final group is that of Jews who do not identify with any of these forms of Judaism, holding a variety of religious beliefs or none, yet still consider themselves Jewish. They account for 29% of U.S. Jews.

Jewish-Christian Relations

The history of the relationship between the Jewish and Christian communities has been a complex one.

In the first few decades after the death of Jesus, Christianity was seen as a new sect within Judaism, one that consisted of those Jews who believed Jesus to have been the Messiah. This would make it no anomaly at the time - every few years a new pretender to the title of Messiah would emerge with his group of followers. Thus the early Christians, almost all of whom were Jews by origin, were seen as "apostate" Jews, and subject to punishment by the Jewish authorities as heretics. And they themselves, too, still saw themselves as Jews, albeit ones who followed the new "way" that was introduced by the Jewish Messiah, Jesus. Hence they continued to participate in many Jewish practices, including synagogue and Temple worship. This only ended definitively around 132 AD, with the emergence of another claimant to the title of Messiah, Bar Kochba. When Bar Kochba called on the Jews to take up arms and violently overthrow their Roman oppressors, the only Jews who refused to participate - because they knew that Jesus, not Bar Kochba, was the true Messiah - were those early Jewish Christians. It was their refusal to participate in the Bar Kochba revolt (which resulted in the final dispersion of Jews from the Holy Land) that led to the definitive separation between the Jewish-Christians and the rest of the Jewish community.

Among the early Jewish Christians there were those who made the error of overemphasizing the continuing need to follow Jewish ritual law even after Jesus - a heresy that came to be known as "judaizing". In response there was a tendency for some early Christian theologians to overreact, with exaggerated polemics condemning Jews and Judaism.

There was a political dimension, too, to the early conflict. The Jewish community had finally achieved a workable relationship with the Roman authorities under whom they lived, and feared that the new Christians - who were perceived by the Roman authorities as another type of Jew - would endanger that relationship. In their favorable treatment of slaves and the poor, the Christians were perceived by those authorities as posing a threat to the social order.

With rare exceptions, a contentious relationship between the Jewish and Christian communities continued throughout most of the ensuing centuries. The causes for the tension included social, economic, theological, political, and spiritual ones. The Jews were visibly outsiders, a separateness emphasized by their distinctive dress, customs, dietary and religious practices dictated by Jewish law. The mere continued visible existence of the Jews seemed to be an insult to the truth of Christianity. This perception was exacerbated by the fact that in their rejection of the claims of Christianity, the Talmud and other Jewish theological books contained insults and blasphemies against Jesus and the Blessed Virgin Mary.

Social and economic factors also contributed to the tension. In many Christian countries Jews were forbidden from owning land or engaging in trades, leaving them little alternative than to support themselves by buying and selling. As such, they were seen as making a parasitic living off the productive work of others. Since Christian religious principles were often seen as prohibiting Christians from lending money at interest, banking activities fell to the Jews, which could also lead to resentment. Once the Jews became a powerful economic force, it frequently was to the political or economic advantage of Christian leaders to incite animosity, or even violence, against them.

One theological factor that contributed to the tension between the two communities was the understanding of the Church teaching "extra ecclesiam nulla salus", i.e. "outside the Church there is no salvation". Until the 20th century, this Church doctrine was understood to mean that anyone who died without formally being a member of the Catholic Church was damned. In such a context, almost any pressure - including violence - that was exerted on the Jews to convert could be seen, in fact, as an act of charity, since if they persisted in their "stubbornness" they were certain to be damned.

The shift in the understanding of that doctrine that took place in the 20th century did much to take the pressure off the relationship between the two communities, and to allow them to see each other in a much more benign light. The Church's current understanding of that doctrine is presented in paragraph 14 of the Vatican II document *Lumen Gentium* (repeated in the *Catechism of the Catholic Church* para. 847):

> Those who, through no fault of their own, do not know the Gospel of Christ or his Church, but who nevertheless seek God with a sincere heart, and, moved by grace, try in their actions to do his will as they know it through the dictates of their conscience - those too may achieve eternal salvation.

Vatican II thus ushered in a new era in Jewish-Christian relations, characterized by a far more positive interaction than ever before. It came, however, at the cost of the cessation of most of the Church's activity, including prayer, aimed at evangelizing Jews.

Judaism from a Catholic Perspective

The Jews' Role Prior to the 1ˢᵗ Coming of Christ

As mentioned at the outset, according to the Catholic faith Judaism has played an absolutely central role in bringing about the salvation of all mankind. It was Jesus himself who said, "salvation is from the Jews" (*Jn* 4:22).

The role Judaism played over the first phase of salvation history, from the creation of man until the Incarnation, is actually quite straightforward. When man was first created, he was to live in a state of uninterrupted bliss and intimacy with God for all eternity. When Adam sinned, that initial state was shattered, and from that very moment - actually, even before then, since God is outside time - God knew that He would someday restore man to an even higher state through the future incarnation of the Second Person of the Most Holy Trinity as a man. If the Second Person of the most Holy Trinity was to incarnate as a man, it would be at a particular point in time and among a particular, "chosen" people. That people have to be prepared over many centuries. First, they would have to be separated from all of the other tribes around them who worshiped fallen spirits - i.e. demons - masquerading as gods. They would have to learn about and worship the one true God, the uncreated

Creator of all that is. They would have to be taught about the creation and fall of man, the seriousness of sin, the need for redemption, and the coming of a Redeemer. They would have to be taught to adhere to a sufficiently high moral code that the Incarnation itself would not be a sacrilege. They would have to be given sufficient divine revelation to be able to recognize the Redeemer when he came; and to be able to spread knowledge of his redemption to the rest of the world after he died. Finally, they would have to prepare, over the generations, a virgin of such purity and holiness that she could give her flesh and blood to be the flesh and blood of the God-man (the Blessed Virgin Mary). That was the role for which the Jews were chosen, and at which they succeeded, despite their widespread failure to follow him. They were chosen to bring about the coming of the Redeemer, and he came, and they were chosen to spread the Gospel to the four corners of the earth, and it has been spread. There could hardly be about 2 billion Christians in the world (of which about 1 billion Catholics), had they failed.

Why the Chosen People

Why did God choose the Jews for this special role, the most important exalted role ever given to any one people? There are many answers to this question. One is that He had to choose somebody, and whoever that was, we would now be asking why He chose *them*. Another is that

God seems to like to choose the weakest and most insignificant for His special missions, precisely to make it apparent that God is behind all that is happening, not the individuals involved. For instance, St Bernadette, the illiterate peasant girl who received the apparitions of the Blessed Virgin Mary at Lourdes, said that "The Holy Virgin chose me because I was the most ignorant of creatures". And when St Margaret Mary Alacoque, the nun chosen to receive the Sacred Heart apparitions, asked Jesus why he chose her for the apparitions, Jesus replied, "Oh that's simple, if I could have found anyone more insignificant than you, I would have chosen her instead." The fact God's choice of the Jews was related to their insignificance is made explicit in the Old Testament:

> "Thus says the Lord God to Jerusalem... On the day you were born, your naval string was not cut, nor were you washed with water to cleanse you nor rubbed with salt nor swathed with bands. ... And when I passed you by, and saw you weltering in your blood, I said to you in your blood, live! ... Then I bathed you with water and washed off your blood, and anointed you with oil. I clothed you with embroidered cloth and shod you with leather. I swathed you with fine linen and covered you with silk... And your renown went forth among the nations because of your beauty, for it was perfect

through the splendor which I had bestowed upon you, says the Lord God." (*Ezk* 16:4-14)

Yet there is also a positive reason why God chose the Jews. He chose the Jews in part to reward Abraham for the extraordinary fidelity he showed in his willingness to sacrifice his son Isaac on Mount Moriah. The story is told in the book of Genesis:

After these things God tested Abraham, and said to him, "Abraham!..." And he said, "Here am I." He said, "Take your son, your only son Isaac, whom you love, and go to the land of Moriah, and offer him there as a burnt offering upon one of the mountains of which I shall tell you." So Abraham rose early in the morning, and took his son Isaac, and went to the place of which God had told him. And Abraham took the wood of the burnt offering, and laid it on Isaac his son; and he took in his hand the fire and the knife. So they went both of them together. And Isaac said to his father Abraham, "I see the fire and the wood; but where is the lamb for a burnt offering?" Abraham said, "God will himself provide the lamb for the sacrifice, my son." When they came to the place of which God had told him, Abraham built an altar there, and laid the wood in order, and bound Isaac his son, and laid him on the altar, upon the wood. Then Abraham put forth his hand, and took the knife to slay his son. But the angel of the LORD called to him from heaven, and said, "Abraham, Abraham!" And he said, "Here am I." He said, "Do not lay your hand on the lad or do anything to him; for now I know that you fear God, seeing you have not withheld your son, your only son, from me."

And Abraham lifted up his eyes and saw a ram, caught in a thicket by his horns; and Abraham went and took the ram, and offered it up as a burnt offering instead of his son. So Abraham called the name of that place "the LORD will provide". And the angel of the LORD called to Abraham a second time from heaven, and said, "Because you have done this, and have not withheld your son, your only son, I will indeed bless you, and I will multiply your descendants as the stars of heaven and as the sand which is on the seashore. And your seed shall possess the gate of their enemies, and in your seed shall all the nations of the earth be blessed, because you have obeyed my voice." (*Gn* 22:1-18, condensed)

This event is central to Christianity and its Christological import can hardly be overstated. Abraham's willingness to sacrifice Isaac was intimately linked to, one could even say reciprocated by, God's willingness, two thousand years later, to sacrifice His only-begotten Son on the very same mountain, just a few hundred yards away, at

the spot known as "Calvary". The very circumstances of
Abraham's act foreshadowed, that is reflected in advance,
the ultimate fulfillment two thousand years later. "Take
your son, your only son, whom you love" (*Gn* 22:2) was
echoed two thousand years later in "For God so loved the
world that he gave his only Son ... [His] beloved Son" (*Jn*
3:16, *Mt* 3:17). As the son of Abraham climbed the mount
with the wood on his shoulders for his own execution, so
too did the Son of God. Abraham's utterance "God
himself will provide the lamb for a burnt offering" (*Gn*
22:8) was prophetic far beyond anything he could have
known, referring not only to the provision of the ram
"provided" by the Lord, but referring far more profoundly
to the only truly acceptable sacrifice, the "Lamb of God,
who took away the sins of the world" (*Jn* 1) - God's own
Son offered on the altar of Calvary.

The "Chosen People"
to Foreshadow Later Salvation History

Salvation history began with Israel, therefore all those
who have later become part of that history have looked
back to the events in Israel's past and seen in them the
prefiguration of later events.

The story of Abraham and Isaac is a prime example of
this role of the Jews - to typologically foreshadow later
salvation history in their own history as a people. Other
examples abound, and were often discussed at length by

the Church fathers. For instance, Judith's cutting off the head of the enemy leader Holofernes (the Book of Judith) was seen as a picture of the Blessed Virgin Mary crushing the head of the serpent, and Esther's interceding before the throne of King Ahasuerus and thus saving the Jewish nation (the Book of Esther) was seen as a picture of the Blessed Virgin Mary's intercession for all before the throne of God.

Particularly significant from a Catholic perspective is the typological foreshadowing of the Eucharist, in the manna given to the Jews in the desert. In fact, the entire story of the Jews' exodus from Egypt was seen by the Church fathers as a summary of salvation through Christ. As St Cyril of Jerusalem, one of the Church Fathers, wrote in his "First Lecture On The Mysteries":

"Let us now teach you the effect wrought upon you on that evening of your baptism....When Pharaoh, that most bitter and cruel tyrant, was oppressing the free and high-born people of the Hebrews, God sent Moses to bring them out of the evil bondage of the Egyptians. Then the door posts were anointed with the blood of a lamb, that the destroyer might flee from the houses which had the sign of the blood; and the Hebrew people was marvelously delivered. The enemy, however, after their rescue, pursued after them, and saw the sea wondrously parted for them; nevertheless he went on, following close in their footsteps, and was all at once overwhelmed and engulfed in the Red Sea.

Now turn from the old to the new, from the figure to the reality. There we have Moses sent from God to Egypt; here, Christ, sent forth from His Father into the world: there, that Moses might lead forth an afflicted people out of Egypt; here, that Christ might rescue those who are oppressed in the world under sin: there, the blood of a lamb was the spell against the destroyer; here, the blood of the Lamb without blemish Jesus Christ is made the charm to scare evil spirits: there, the tyrant was pursuing that ancient people even to the sea; and here the daring and shameless spirit, the author of evil, was following thee even to the very streams of salvation. The tyrant of old was drowned in the sea; and this present one disappears in the water of salvation."

Thus we see that the crossing of the Red Sea, to pass from slavery to freedom, prefigured the Christian's baptism freeing him from original sin; the Blood of the Lamb on the doorpost turning away the avenging angel and sparing the Jews from death prefigured the Blood of Christ on the Cross turning away God's condemnation to eternal death; the forty years journey in the wilderness until reaching the "promised Land" was a "type" of one's lifetime on earth until reaching the true "Promised Land," the "Heavenly Jerusalem"; and the manna with which God miraculously fed the Jews in the desert prefigured the true bread of life, the Eucharist, the heavenly food which nourishes the faithful during their pilgrimage on earth. Jesus himself drew the parallel: (*Jn* 6:48-49, 51):

> "I am the bread of life. Your fathers ate the manna in the wilderness, and they died... I am the living bread which came down from heaven; if any one eats of this bread, he will live for ever; and the bread which I shall give for the life of the world is my flesh."

Finally, the Paschal lamb, sacrificed on that first Passover night in Egypt, was but a figure of the true Paschal Lamb, Jesus sacrificed on Calvary. As St Augustine said (*Contra Faustum Manichaeum*):

> ...[what was thus prefigured in] the feast of the paschal lamb ... has been fulfilled in the sufferings of Christ, the Lamb without spot.... In the gospel we have the true Lamb, not in shadow, but in substance; and instead of prefiguring the death, we commemorate it daily [in the holy sacrifice of the Mass].

This linkage between the Jewish Passover and manna in the desert with the Crucifixion and the Eucharist is given even greater depth when one considers that the last supper was a Passover seder, and the crucifixion took place at the very moment that the Passover lambs were being slaughtered in the Temple. One can consider that the Old Covenant ended, and the New Covenant began, at the very moment that Jesus took the unleavened bread at the Passover seder Christians know as the Last Supper, raised it, and turned it into the first Eucharist with the words "This is my body which is given for you. Do this in remembrance of me" (*Lk* 22:19).

The Jews' Role between the First and Second Comings of Christ

The role that Judaism and the Jewish people have to play in salvation *after* the first coming of Christ is less obvious. Was their role exhausted in bringing about the first coming? Were they as the chosen people entirely replaced by the Church as the "new Israel"? Was their election withdrawn from them, as a consequence of their failure to recognize Christ as the Messiah? Is their continuing failure to recognize Jesus as the Messiah a punishment for their role in the crucifixion? Will they be around until the end of the world (the Second Coming)? Will they have a role to play in the Second Coming, as they had in the First?

A full exploration of these questions is beyond the scope of this work (the interested reader is referred to the author's lengthier work, *Salvation is from the Jews: The Role of Judaism in Salvation History from Abraham to the Second Coming*, published by Ignatius Press), but substantial light can be shed by a brief look at chapter 11 of St Paul's letter to the Romans. Such a look will serve as the conclusion of this book.

Paul's Letter to the Romans:

"I ask, then, has God rejected his people? By no means!...God has not rejected his people whom he foreknew..." (vv. 1-2)

Here is a flat assertion that despite the Jews' rejection of Jesus, they have not been rejected by God. 'This letter was written, of course, well after the crucifixion, and after the Jews stubbornly resisted the Gospel.' As St Paul adds later in the chapter v. 28-29:

"As regards the gospel they are enemies of God, for your sake; but as regards election they are beloved for the sake of their forefathers. For the gifts and the call of God are irrevocable."

Hence, in at least some way, we know that the election of the Jews continues despite rejection of Jesus.

"What then? Israel failed to obtain what it sought. The elect obtained it, but the rest were hardened, as it is written, "God gave them a spirit of stupor, eyes that should not see and ears that should not hear, down to this very day..." (vv. 7-8)

Here St Paul is asserting that God actually veiled the eyes of at least some of the Jews so that they would not recognize Jesus, "down to this very day". What could the reason be? Paul provides the answer:

"Have they stumbled so as to fall? By no means! But through their trespass salvation has come to the Gentiles, so as to make Israel jealous. Now if their trespass means riches for the world, and if their failure means riches for the Gentiles, how much more will their full inclusion mean!" (vv. 11-12)

The suggestion is that the failure of the Jews to recognize Christ was necessary in order for Christianity to spread throughout the Gentile world, and that once that has happened, it will make the Jews jealous, inspiring them too to recognize Christ. We see this same idea, that the Jews' failure to recognize Christ was in order to enable Christianity to spread to the Gentiles, in verse 28, already cited: "As regards the gospel they are enemies of God, for your sake".

Paul seems to have been considering the impediment that would have been imposed on the spread of Christianity if the Jews had accepted Jesus. Christianity could have been seen as a sect within Judaism intended primarily for Jews. In fact, this was an early danger in the Church. Acts 15 recounts the first Church council, called about 18 years after the crucifixion, that was convened to formally determine whether Gentiles could become Christians without first having to become Jews - in other words, whether Christianity was for everyone, or just for Jews. This danger was greatly lessened by the Jews' widespread failure to respond to the Gospel. As St Paul put it, "Their failure", that is to recognize Christ, meant "riches for the Gentiles", i.e. facilitated the spread of Christianity to the Gentiles.

Yet St Paul immediately continues with the suggestion that this failure will not be permanent, and when the Jews do enter the Church, they will bring a special blessing to it:

> "...if their failure means riches for the Gentiles, how much more will their full inclusion mean!...For if their rejection means the reconciliation of the world, what will their acceptance mean but life from the dead? (vv. 12-15)

Paul continues:

"If the dough offered as first fruits is holy, so is the whole lump; and if the root is holy, so are the branches. But if some of the branches were broken off, and you, a wild olive shoot, were grafted in their place to share the richness of the olive tree, do not boast over the branches. Remember it is not you that support the root, but the root that supports you. You will say, "Branches were broken off so that I might be grafted in." That is true. [But] even the others, if they do not persist in their unbelief, will be grafted in, for God has the power to graft them in again. For if you have been cut from what is by nature a wild olive tree, and grafted, contrary to nature, into a cultivated olive tree, how much more will these natural branches be grafted back into their own olive tree." (vv. 16-24)

Here Paul is reminding his Gentile listeners not to feel superior to the Jews on the basis of the Jews' failure to recognize Christ. The Jews were the natural branches growing on the olive tree of salvation; some were broken off - the Jews who rejected Jesus - to make room for the grafting in of wild olive branches (the Gentiles), but that is no reason for the grafted-in wild branches to boast. For the cultivated branches - the Jews - will later be grafted back in (when the Jews later enter the Church), at which time they will be even better suited to the tree - salvation through Christ - than the Gentiles, for they had originally been a part of it.

When will this happen? Paul continues:

"I want you to understand this mystery, brethren: a hardening has come upon part of Israel, until the full number of the Gentiles come in, and so all Israel will be saved." (vv. 25-26)

The veil that has been cast over the eyes of the Jews will be lifted, and they too will recognize Christ, when the "full number of the Gentiles" has come in. What does that refer to? This idea of the "times of the Gentiles" which ends only after the "full number of the Gentiles come in" appears in a prophecy made by Jesus himself, shortly before the crucifixion, in which he said:

"They [the Jews] will fall by the edge of the sword and be led captive among all nations, and Jerusalem will be trodden down by the Gentiles, until the times of the Gentiles are fulfilled, and there will be signs in sun and moon and stars and upon the earth distress of nations and perplexity of roaring of the sea and the waves, men fainting with fear and with foreboding of what is coming on the world, for the powers of the Heavens will be shaken, and then they will see the Son of Man coming in a cloud with great Glory." (*Lk* 21:24-27)

The Jews literally fell by the edge of the sword and were led captive among all nations when Jerusalem fell to the Romans, first in 70 AD and then for the final time in 135 AD. From that point on Jerusalem was "trodden down by the Gentiles", i.e. in Gentile hands, until 1967 AD, at which point the old city of Jerusalem returned to Jewish hands for the first time in almost 2000 years. Jesus' prophecy then continues with a vivid description of the Second Coming.

Thus the "times of the Gentiles" seems to refer to the period between the First Coming of Christ, and a time shortly preceding the Second Coming. During this epoch the Jews will, by and large, reject Jesus as the Messiah, leaving the way open for the Gentiles to enter, and dominate the Church. Once the "full number of the gentiles" has come in, the veil will be lifted from the eyes of the Jews, and they too will recognize Jesus, entering the Church in great numbers. In so doing, their "full inclusion" will mean "great riches" for the Church, "bringing life from the dead". Shortly thereafter Christ will return in glory, to a Church now completed by the [re]entry of the Jews (the original olive branches, broken off to make room for the wild branches, the Gentiles, to be grafted in). The Catechism of the Catholic Church explicitly associates this prophesied conversion of the Jews with the Second Coming:

The glorious Messiah's coming is suspended at every moment of history until his recognition by "all Israel", for "a hardening has come upon part of Israel" in their "unbelief" toward Jesus [*Rm* 11:20-26; cf. *Mt* 23:39] ...The "full inclusion" of the Jews in the Messiah's salvation, in the wake of "the full number of the Gentiles" will enable the People of God to achieve "the measure of the stature of the fullness of Christ" [*Rm* 11:12, 25; cf. *Lk* 21:24], in which "God may be all in all" [*Ep* 4:13; 1 *Co* 15:2]. (*CCC* 674)

Given this glorious future for the Church, Jew and Gentile, one can do no better than to conclude this brief study with the words with which St Paul closes Romans 11:

Just as you [the Gentiles] were once disobedient to God but now have received mercy because of their [the Jews'] disobedience, so they [the Jews] have now been disobedient in order that by the mercy shown to you they also may receive mercy. For God has consigned all men to disobedience, that he may have mercy upon all.

O the depth of the riches and wisdom and knowledge of God! How unsearchable are his judgments and how inscrutable his ways! "For who has known the mind of the Lord, or who has been his counselor? Or who has given a gift to him that he might be repaid?" For from him and through him and to him are all things. To him be glory for ever. Amen. (*Rm* 11:33-36)

Further Reading

Additional information on this topic can be found on the author's website *www.salvationisfromthejews.com* and in his books *Salvation is from the Jews: The Role of Judaism in Salvation History from Abraham to the Second Coming* (Ignatius 2003), and *Honey from the Rock: Sixteen Jews Find the Sweetness of Christ* (Ignatius 2007). He also may be contacted directly at *schoeman@catholic.org*

ENDNOTES

[1] John Paul II's visit to the Great Synagogue of Rome 13 April, 1986.

[2] John Paul II address on the fiftieth anniversary of the Warsaw Ghetto Uprising, 6 April, 1993.

[3] John Paul II's address to the Jewish Community in Mainz, West Germany, 17 November, 1980.

[4] Vatican II, *Dogmatic Constitution On Divine Revelation Dei Verbum*, 18 November, 1965.

[5] *ibid.*, para 16.

[6] Vatican II, *Nostra Aetate*, 1965, para. 4.

[7] From Rabbi Schneerson's introduction to Schneur Zalman of Liadi's *Tanya*, English translation (Brooklyn, N.Y. Kehot Publication Society, 1962), p. vii.

[8] e.g. *Dn* 9:24-27; *Gn* 49:10; *Is* 6:9-10, 7:14, 9:1-6, 11:1-4, 35:4-7, 40:3-5, 53:1-12, 61:1-2; *Jr* 23:5; *Ml* 3:1; *Mi* 5:2; *Nb* 24:17; *Ps* 22, 34, 72:1-11; *2 S* 7:12-13; *Ws* 2:12-24; *Zc* 9:9, 12:10.

[9] The *tzitzit* come from Numbers 15:38-40: "Speak to the people of Israel, and bid them to make tassels on the corners of their garments throughout their generations, and to put upon the tassel of each corner a cord of blue; and it shall be to you a tassel to look upon and remember all the commandments of the LORD, to do them, not to follow after your own heart and your own eyes, which you are inclined to go after wantonly. So you shall remember and do all my commandments, and be holy to your God."

[10] The law requiring beards and earlocks is found in Leviticus 19:27: "You shall not round off the hair on your temples or mar the edges of your beard."

[11] Our calendar is a "solar" calendar. It maintains a precise synchronization with the earth's orbit around the sun, but ignores the moon's orbit around the earth; as a consequence, the new moon may fall on any day of the month. By contrast, the Jewish calendar is a "solar-lunar" calendar, based both on the earth's orbit around the sun and on the moon's rotation around the earth, such that every month begins with a new moon. In order to achieve this, the number of days in the year varies slightly from year to year. Because of this, from year to year Jewish festivals fall on different days of the Western calendar.

[12] Exodus 12:13; the overall story of Passover is told in Exodus 2-15.

[13] The percentages in this section are from studies done by in the U.S. and Israel. The U.S. figures would be roughly representative of the Jewish population in the U.K. and Western Europe, too.

[14] Many Jews who come to faith in Christ do not consider that they have "converted" at all, but rather feel they remain as Jewish as ever - or more so, since now they are followers of the Jewish Messiah. The term is adopted here for ease of use.

[15] *Voices of Messianic Judaism*, Dan Cohn-Sherbok ed., Lederer Books, Baltimore MD, 2001, pp. 12ff.

[16] Sheri Ross Gordon, "Inside Jews for Jesus", Reform Judaism, 22 (Winter 1993), 24, cited in William Greene, PhD., The Ascendance of Messianic Judaism in the Context of Hebrew Christianity, taken from the internet.

[17] Jewish Community Relations Council of New York, *www.jcrcny.org*.